Table of Contents:

Introduction:

I'm sure a lot of women will hate me for writing this book because I'm going to tell the truth. Before writing this book, I talked to a lot of women, from different cultures and backgrounds. I also drew on my own experience and concluded that yes, women do like bad boys. It's unfair to good men, I know. Freud spent his life studying women and at the end of his days, he failed to understand what women are really looking for. Most men think it's almost impossible to understand women and that there's no point in wasting their time. It's true that women do weird things sometimes, rejecting nice, considerate guys in the friend zone for example. But women aren't as hard to understand as men think. If you're looking to increase your success with women, you'd better understand how their emotions work and how these emotions influence their decisions. The best way to understand women and know exactly what they want is to focus your attention on their actions, not their words.

A woman will tell you that she's tired of falling for assholes, that she's tired of men cheating on her, that she's looking for a good man and.... Two days later, she's back in the arms of her toxic ex who was also a cheater. That's why I decided to write this book, to help you understand women and be more attractive to them.

The nice guy

Ever since you were a kid, your mom told you that you had to be a nice guy. Especially with women. She explained that the best way to seduce a woman is to buy her flowers, chocolate or write her a poem. Years later, you've followed all her advice, but you're still single. You wonder what the reason could be since you're much more in tune with women than most of the men you know. You are genuinely kind and caring with women. You treat women like princesses. What if you're too nice? What if your mother lied to you? Being nice is a beautiful quality. I'd never advise you to become an asshole in order to seduce women and get them into bed. However, there's a difference between being nice and being TOO nice. Women often say that the first quality they look for in a man is kindness. But it's FALSE.

Women often say the exact opposite of what they mean. They say they're looking for a nice guy, but they always end up with the wrong guys, whom they then describe as "assholes". Don't listen to women, understand them. A woman doesn't fall in love with a guy because he's nice. A woman needs to be seduced. And niceness is not a discriminating factor in seduction. If you're only nice, you'll end up in the "boyfriend" or "friend" box. It's important to understand one thing: being nice because you feel it in the moment is not a problem. On the other hand, being nice in order to get feedback and recognition, and to be loved by the other person, is false, manipulative and unnatural. It's not by being nice to women that you'll win them over. True kindness is an act of pure generosity without any expectations of the other person.

Here are some signs that you're too nice to women:

- You constantly apologize

- You never say "No" to them. You always agree with them.

- You're always available for them. It doesn't matter what time of day it is.

- You give too many compliments

- You double-text if they don't text you back.

- You use your money to get their attention

- You put too much value on a female for no reason

Do you recognize yourself in at least one of these things? It's time to change your attitude.

What is a bad boy?

Before giving the reasons why we, women, like bad boys, I think it's important to define a bad boy. The bad boy isn't necessarily the one portrayed in books or movies. He's not that tattooed man with piercings, super hot, a drinker, sometimes a drug addict or a seducer. These are clichés we've ingrained in our heads. The bad boy is more of a male, or rather an "alpha male". Bad boys don't change who they are in hopes of making anyone like them, they really do believe they're good enough. He's not the "bad guy". He's the one who does what he wants, takes responsibility for his actions, and has a quirky personality. The bad boy has an attitude which is typical of him and which sets him apart from other men. And that's where his charm lies, and why women are attracted to him.

For a woman, a bad boy is a man who doesn't like us and who's going to hurt us. We know very well that this boy isn't right for us and that he's not going to treat us the way we'd like.

However, even if he treats us badly and doesn't offer us love, we want to make him fall in love with us. We know that his exes haven't managed to change him, and we like the idea of thinking that we're going to do better than the other women from his past. We want him to be different with us. Bad boys represent everything we love, everything that seems interesting, risky, dangerous and different. We're well aware that they'll disappear overnight without a trace, that they'll leave with someone else, but we still like them. You never know what to expect, he hardly ever answers our calls or texts, sometimes he's very close to us, sometimes very distant. We women are contradictory. We don't go for men we say we like. We often tell our friends and family that we're looking for a "good man who will love and respect us" but unfortunately, this is not the case.

Women are only looking for this kind of man when they're older. They look for a good man when they want to have children, when they want some stability, and that's when they realize that those men they used to reject in the friendzone are now all happily married.

In general, a woman finds it easy to meet and seduce men (you know the reason). That's why she's so picky. She doesn't take the time to answer messages or give "too nice" men a chance. She friendzones them. And it has nothing to do with their physical appearance. Women want to earn a man's affection. If we feel we got it too easily or that he's more invested than we are, we lose interest.

Why are women attracted to bad boys?

There are several reasons why women are attracted to a bad boy:

- His charisma: Bad boys have character, they assert themselves. They are dominant and seductive. They have certain alpha traits. They're also very self-confident. They're unbelievably self-assured and outspoken. Bad boys know what they want and stand by their choices. He likes to have the last word on almost everything, and knows how to defend and impose his ideas. He's so sure of himself that he's not afraid to take risks. Hence his success with women.
- His unattainability: Have you ever noticed that we humans are attracted to things we can't have? What we've already got can tire us out very quickly.

It's the "follow me, I'll run away from you, run away from me, I'll follow you" principle, and it applies to relationships too.

Women generally like a challenge. A bad boy is a daily challenge for a woman. Women are always attracted to difficulty, because they also want to seduce. Most women are attracted to the novelty and challenge of pursuing someone they can't have. The idea of achieving or obtaining what seems difficult or unattainable can be exciting and motivating for them. The bad boy understood long ago that he had to run away to be followed by women. When you distance yourself from a woman, you become less available to her, which can make you appear scarce or rare. She will be drawn to you because she perceives you as a novelty or challenge. Human beings are naturally curious. When you keep some distance or maintain an air of mystery, it can pique people's curiosity.

They may want to get to know you better to uncover what makes you tick. Some women are attracted to the idea of pursuing a man who seems unattainable or distant.

They view it as a challenge and want to prove to themselves that they can win your attention or affection. This can boost their self-esteem.When you analyze everything more closely, you realize that you men are the same way too. You guys like women who are difficult to seduce, you like challenges.When a woman is too easy to get, you quickly lose interest.

- Women don't know what they want: many women really don't know what they're looking for. As a result, they multiply toxic relationships. Our romantic choices often get shaped by our personal history and past experiences. So, when some women seem to have trouble figuring out what they really want in a partner, it might be connected to things that happened in their past. Maybe they didn't have the best experiences with their dad or something else that influenced their ideas about love. These past experiences can play a big role in what they're looking for in a relationship, and sometimes, it leads to getting stuck in not-so-healthy patterns.

- The idea that they can change him: In many cases, women fall in love with bad boys because they think they can change them. Many women have the false impression that they can correct a bad boy's tendencies and turn him into the caring, considerate, committed person they want him to become. They want to feel that they are an exception to this man, that they are different in his eyes. They genuinely think they're special, different from everyone else who's tried and failed to change this person.

- Women's hormones: Hormones decide for us women!

Hormones influence our behavior, our weight, our thoughts and our impulses. It's the same story for that inexplicable attraction to bad boys, and it's scientifically proven.

In fact, a study by the University of Texas has managed to prove a correlation between these attractions and women's hormones. Kristina Durante, who led the research, explains that when "women are in the midst of ovulation, they feel more attracted to good-looking guys". Why? Because "the hormones associated with fertility lead them to have illusions about these types of men, and to think that they could be devoted partners and better fathers".

How to be irresistible in a woman's eyes?

As I mentioned before, women are generally attracted to men who are inaccessible, who have lots of women in their lives and who don't give them much attention. Unfortunately, they reject nice guys who make a lot of effort to please them, who respect them and are there for them. Yes, life is unfair and we women are evil creatures for doing this to nice men. But we mustn't forget that men do the same thing to women. Human beings are complicated: they're always attracted by the unattainable, they like to chase after things they can't control, and they're always trying to control the uncontrollable. The unattainable always seems more seductive and more attractive, because you have to work so hard to get it. When a person isn't sure of getting something, he or she won't stop thinking about it, and the more he or she thinks about it, the more he or she will invest in it, the more attached he or she will become to it, and the harder he or she will find it to forget about it.

If everyone can get something effortlessly, it means it's not really worth much and doesn't deserve much effort to get it. On the other hand, if something is difficult or inaccessible to most people, being the only ones to have it will give us enormous satisfaction and an ego boost. Women are used to having men who are far too interested from the start. For them, all men are the same. There's no suspense. On the other hand, if a woman finds a guy who hasn't shown much interest from the start, she's going to wonder why. Then she's going to do everything she can to get that man to be interested, and to get that man to be like other men. That's why this woman will do everything she can to get him. She's even going to start chasing him. Just because she can't have him, she'll do anything to get him. Sometimes you have to push a woman away to attract her. If you show yourself unattainable, you'll be seen differently from all the other guys who are at the feet of this woman you want to seduce. You'll become an obsession for her.

So the next time you interact with a woman who constantly rejects other guys, make sure you show yourself unapproachable.

Become less available:

This technique works with all women, but especially with pretty, unattainable women. It works less with ordinary women, who are less attractive. On the contrary, it risks repelling them even more and making them lose interest. Because if a woman realizes that you're too unapproachable and that she doesn't stand a chance with you no matter how hard she tries to please you, she'll give up and move on to another man who'll be more accessible and who'll be able to give her what she wants. So it's up to you to find the right balance to seduce the woman you like. You mustn't be too accessible or too inaccessible. This technique of being "less available" only applies with pretty women who know they're beautiful and have lots of guys at their feet. Women like to chase after unavailable guys, even if they pretend otherwise and say they prefer guys who make them priorities in life.

We women don't use logic to choose our partners. If a man doesn't give a woman too much interest, she'll unconsciously try to find out why this man isn't chasing after her like other guys. We question ourselves and wonder why he doesn't give us the attention we're used to receiving from other men. Rarity increases value. A woman assumes that a man who is too available and quickly falls in love with her probably doesn't have many options with women. Women like unapproachable men. Why is that? We want to test our seductive powers. Our ego comes into play. Bad boys are a challenge because once she's managed to seduce him, it'll be hard for another woman to come along and snatch him away. A man who can't keep a lid on things and reveals all his cards easily will never be very interesting to women. Life with a predictable man will be monotonous, tasteless and, above all, boring. Human beings in general like to control the uncontrollable and chase after what escapes them. Women are competitive creatures and will do anything for a good man. In other words, women are elitist creatures, attracted to the most dominant males and the most sought-after by other women.

You can't do anything to change them, because they're genetically programmed to behave that way. On the other hand, you can change your behavior and become better, more dominant, stronger and women will become more submissive and docile with you. The bad boy has a strong character. He shows that he's independent and doesn't need a woman to survive. But don't confuse these characteristics with meanness. Women hate bad/mean men.

Being a bad boy doesn't mean being disrespectful to a woman. A bad boy is a man who shows kindness while maintaining a position of dominance. He's a man who behaves in this way to please, not to harm, a woman. He plays this game to attract women's attention. He recognizes the value and importance of women.

A little advice would be to remain a good person, while

retaining a certain degree of mystery. Don't be unapproachable, but if you're too available, it's likely to bore your conquest. If you say yes to everything, they'll tire of it very quickly. That's why bad boys are so successful in this area. They're not always available, they're not always the most attentive, and so it becomes a habit.

Stop doing these things:

I'm now going to give you a list of all the things you should stop doing if you want to be irresistible to women and stop being friendzoned.

Stop over-complimenting them:

YES, women love compliments. The more attention and compliments we receive, the more powerful we feel. But that doesn't mean that if you compliment us, you'll create attraction. Beautiful women are used to receiving compliments all the time. If you compliment her, you'll be like every other man who appreciates her for her physical beauty. You need to stand out. For example, your first message/DM to a woman should never be a compliment about her physical beauty. Men who are too nice tend to give far too many compliments, especially about looks.

If you want to seduce a woman, you'll have to give fewer compliments, or even avoid giving them at all, especially if you've just met her. A woman already knows she's beautiful. Lots of men tell her that all the time. Women love the chase. Be mysterious. Awaken her intrigue and let her take an interest in you. Let her hunt you. When a woman knows she can have you, she doesn't want you. I didn't say never to compliment a woman.

On a date, you can compliment her on a particular part of her outfit: she'll have made the effort to dress well and deserves the compliment. But be careful: too many compliments can spoil the fun. Your compliments must be rare, because everything that's rare has value. The other problem with giving a woman too many compliments is that she'll start to think she's too good for you. If you start a conversation with a woman by saying "You're too beautiful. I'm not pretty enough for you", you're shooting yourself in the foot.

Don't try to buy a woman affection:

You can not buy attraction. When a man tries to buy a woman's affection with food and gifts, he may come across to women as being over-compensating for his insecurity. Giving an expensive or overly extravagant gift early in a relationship or before a mutual emotional connection is established can sometimes give the impression of rushing or trying too hard to win someone over. It's essential to consider the timing and context of gift-giving. Continually giving gifts without receiving any emotional or material investment in return may lead to perceptions of desperation. Healthy relationships involve mutual give-and-take. You will not make a woman attracted to you by buying her a gift. No matter how expensive the gift is.

Don't be available every time SHE wants to hang out.

If she really liked you, she'd like to see you at a time that's convenient for both of you. Not just for her. If she cancels an appointment and offers to reschedule, don't accept directly. You also need to tell her when YOU are free. You have to show her that your needs are important too. If every time she cancels and reschedules you accept, she'll think she can cancel the appointment at any time and she'll know you'll still be interested. You have to show her that you don't deal with this type of behavior.When you're not constantly available, it can create an air of mystery. People are naturally curious, and they may wonder what you're doing or why you're not always at their beck and call. This intrigue can make you more appealing. Not always being available sends a message that your time is valuable and that you have other priorities and interests in your life. This can make you seem more desirable because you're seen as someone who is well-rounded and has a life outside of the relationship.

Don't plan everything around her.

Planning everything around a woman can often reduce attraction in a relationship.

When she becomes the sole focus and her every need and desire are constantly catered to, it can lead to a sense of predictability and emotional suffocation. Over time, the intrigue and excitement that are essential for attraction may diminish as the relationship may start to feel one-sided, with one partner investing too heavily in the other. To keep the flames of attraction alive, it's important to allow room for individuality and personal interests within the relationship, fostering a dynamic where both partners continue to grow and surprise each other.

If you're going out with your friends on Saturday night, don't cancel just to spend time with her.

Stop over apologizing:

This can give the impression that you're willing to subdue your own needs or views to please her, fostering a sense of submission. It's essential to remember that apologizing when it's warranted is a sign of maturity and accountability, but overdoing it can convey a lack of assertiveness and self-assuredness, which can impact the way women perceive your confidence and self-respect. Balancing apologies with self-assurance and not apologizing excessively can help maintain a more balanced and confident presence in your interactions. If you apologize too much, you'll seem submissive. The more you apologize, the more you appear to be afraid of losing the beautiful woman you're flirting with (fear that she'll leave, fear of not attracting her, etc...) Women want men who are at least a little self-assured and who aren't there to stick it to them.

Make women your only motivation:

Focusing all your attention on chasing women and neglecting other parts of your life isn't the best approach. While finding romance is great, it's important to keep a broader perspective. When you put everything on hold just to pursue women, you're missing out on personal growth and the chance to explore other exciting aspects of life, like building a career, hanging out with friends, or working on self-improvement.

Plus, it can create an awkward pressure when you do meet someone you're interested in. If they sense that you're solely focused on finding a partner, it might feel like a lot of weight on the relationship. It's like the old saying, "You can't find love when you're looking for it." Sometimes, the best relationships happen when you least expect them. When you spread your focus across different parts of life, it's not just about keeping busy; it's about becoming a more well-rounded and intriguing person. You bring more to the table when you've got a range of interests and experiences. Plus, having passions and goals outside of romance can make you more confident and attractive to potential partners. So, a balanced life with various interests ensures that your happiness doesn't depend solely on romantic relationships, which ultimately leads to a more fulfilling and enjoyable existence.

Thinking that a woman is doing you a favor by dating you

When you encounter an incredibly attractive woman and you can't help but notice that she is more attractive than you, it's important to acknowledge this reality without letting it undermine your self-esteem. There's nothing wrong with recognizing her beauty, in fact, it's entirely natural.

However, the challenge arises when you take this observation to an extreme by placing her on a pedestal of attractiveness and, in turn, feeling unworthy. This self-doubt can significantly impact your chances of building a connection with her.

In such cases, she is likely to sense your lack of self-assuredness, your belief that she is somehow superior, and your apprehension that she might be doing you a favor by considering you as a potential partner. The truth is, most beautiful women don't want to feel like they're granting a favor by entering a relationship.

They seek a partner who believes he is a strong match for her and possesses the self-confidence to back it up, ideally considering himself not just good enough, but even more than good enough for her.

It's essential to remember that attractiveness goes far beyond looks. Confidence, self-assuredness, and authenticity are qualities that can strongly influence the perception of attractiveness. Instead of fixating on physical appearance, consider the depth of connection, shared interests, and emotional compatibility when pursuing any relationship, as these elements often form the most meaningful and lasting connections.

Start doing these things:

Become more mysterious

Women like mysterious men. Avoid revealing all your cards too quickly to a woman. The idea is always to save a few surprises for the future, things she'll discover about you over time. Avoid revealing too much. What makes a person a mystery is knowing as little as possible about them. If she asks you questions, avoid telling the details, or the whole story. Be vague enough to make her want to know more about you. The problem is that if you guess too early with a woman, whether it's about your feelings for her or your qualities, your passions or your job, there's no mystery left for her. There's nothing left for her to discover. And that makes the relationship much less exciting, because there's no longer the thrill of potential future discoveries.

This is another reason why you shouldn't reveal your feelings too quickly. You can tell her that you like her, but as I mentioned earlier, never tell her that you're into her, that you'd do anything for her... (You can only say these things if you've already been in a relationship for a while). In the case of a woman you've just met, you need to reveal yourself little by little, so as to always maintain a sense of mystery. Because mystery arouses curiosity. Mystery is exciting.

The woman wants to know more about you. And that goes for your activities and qualities too: for example, let's say you're a very good tennis player. Don't tell her straight out! Keep it a mystery. Let her find out for herself when she asks you questions. You want her to feel that there's always something to find out about you. It's a bit like a movie. I doubt you'd want to watch a movie or read a book where you already know the ending.

Take the lead:

Women tend to find it quite appealing when a guy takes the lead and makes decisions, including something as seemingly minor as choosing a restaurant for a date night. It's not about being overbearing or inflexible but rather about displaying confidence and those vital leadership qualities. Some guys might be concerned that making the wrong choice could disappoint their date, which is understandable. However, it's often more unattractive to put the entire decision-making burden on the woman. Women typically appreciate a partner who can take initiative, plan, and guide the way, as it demonstrates a certain level of self-assuredness and independence. Even if your restaurant choice doesn't align perfectly with her preferences, the mere fact that you've taken charge and made a decision shows that you're capable of leadership.

It's not about dictating; it's about asserting your confidence and highlighting your ability to make choices, a quality that's often admired in a man.

So, step up, show some initiative, and let your decisiveness shine through in your dating life. It can be an attractive quality that goes a long way in establishing a strong connection

Be funny

Women are naturally attracted to men with a great sense of humor. It's not just about being funny; it's about radiating good vibes and positivity. A funny guy can turn a dull moment into something unforgettable, and this kind of positivity is super attractive. It shows that he can keep the good times rolling even when life throws curveballs, which is like a beacon for women looking for someone fun and dependable. And confidence? It comes naturally with humor.

A guy who can make people laugh is someone who's comfortable in his own skin, and that's super attractive. Confidence is like a magnet, and a funny guy has that in spades.

Plus, being funny makes you relatable. It's like a secret handshake that opens up connections with people. A good laugh can break the ice and create a connection that's instant and genuine. That feeling of being comfortable and valued is gold in any interaction. A shared laugh is a magic glue that bonds people. When a guy can make a woman laugh, they're not just having a good time; they're making memories and building a deeper connection. And here's the thing: humor is also charismatic. It's like having a superpower that draws people in. Charismatic guys have that special something, and a great sense of humor is usually at the heart of it.

Be confident without being arrogant:

I'm sure you've heard that plenty of times. Confidence is like a magnetic force that draws women in, and it's a quality that holds an irresistible allure. A confident man exudes an air of self-assuredness that is simply captivating. When a woman encounters a man who is confident, she can't help but be intrigued. It's like an unspoken promise of a more fulfilling and enjoyable connection.Confidence signifies that you're comfortable in your own skin, that you know your worth, and that you're unapologetically yourself.

These qualities are incredibly attractive because they convey a sense of security and stability. A confident man isn't just attractive; he's a reliable presence in a woman's life, someone she can lean on and trust. This is a quality that goes beyond just superficial charm.

Confidence also has a powerful impact on how a man carries himself. A confident man tends to have excellent posture, stands tall, and moves with purpose.

This physicality is not only visually appealing but also communicates a strong presence. It's like a silent declaration that you are someone who knows how to navigate life with grace and poise. Moreover, a confident man is also a great communicator. He has no trouble maintaining eye contact and engaging in meaningful conversations. This ability to connect on a deeper level is inherently attractive because it signifies your capacity to form genuine connections and engage emotionally.

Confidence doesn't mean you're free of self-doubt or insecurity; it means you've learned to manage those feelings and not let them define you. A confident man is self-aware, and he uses that awareness to grow and improve. This combination of self-assuredness and self-awareness creates an alluring package.

Women appreciate a man who knows what he wants and isn't afraid to go after it. Confidence often comes with a sense of purpose and ambition, and this drive is incredibly attractive. When a man is confident in his pursuit of his goals, it shows he's passionate, motivated, and committed to making his dreams a reality. This kind of ambition is a potent aphrodisiac.

On the flip side, there's a fine line between confidence and arrogance. While confidence is appealing, arrogance can be a major turn-off. Arrogance often stems from insecurity, whereas true confidence is rooted in self-assuredness. It's important to maintain a humble and respectful attitude, treating others with kindness and consideration.

Confidence is like a secret weapon when it comes to attracting women. It's not just about being attractive; it's about being a reliable, secure, and engaging partner. It's about embracing your flaws and vulnerabilities and using them to grow and become the best version of yourself. When you're confident, you become a person who not only attracts but also deeply connects with women, making you irresistible in their eyes.

Be ambitious

Women are instinctively drawn to men who possess a well-defined sense of purpose and are fueled by an inner drive to achieve their goals. This attraction is deeply rooted in the idea that a man with ambitions not only has a direction in life but also signifies a sense of determination and dedication, qualities that women find irresistibly appealing. To captivate a woman's heart, it's essential to showcase your ambition, demonstrating that you're working towards something that truly matters to you, whether it's climbing the career ladder, pursuing a creative endeavor, or seeking personal growth. Having ambitions isn't just about the destination; it's about the journey, and women often appreciate the vitality and enthusiasm that ambition can bring into a man's life. Women love the idea of being with a partner who inspires them to reach for their own aspirations, creating a dynamic that fosters mutual growth and support.

However, it's essential to remember that when it comes to attracting women, it's not just about talking the talk, but also walking the walk. Your ambitions should manifest in your actions, reflecting your commitment to achieving your goals. Women are naturally attuned to authenticity, and genuine ambition is an attractive quality when it's backed by tangible efforts and progress.

While showcasing your ambitions is important, balance is key. It's crucial to avoid making your aspirations the sole focus of your interactions. Overemphasizing your ambitions can inadvertently come across as self-absorption, which can be off-putting. Instead, aim to strike a balance in your conversations, showing interest in her goals and dreams as well. Sharing and supporting each other's ambitions can create a meaningful connection and strengthen your bond. Women are profoundly drawn to men with a clear sense of direction and ambition. The drive to pursue meaningful goals not only signifies determination but also adds an exciting dimension to your character. When backed by sincere effort and a balanced approach to conversations, your ambitions become a compelling force that can genuinely attract women, creating the potential for a deep and fulfilling connection built on shared dreams and mutual growth.

Take care of your appearance:

Taking care of your appearance is undeniably crucial when it comes to attracting women. It's not about conforming to unrealistic beauty standards; it's about presenting the best version of yourself.

Your appearance is the first thing people notice, and it sets the stage for initial impressions. When you put effort into your appearance, you naturally feel more confident, and this boost in self-esteem is attractive to women.

Confidence is contagious, and a man who feels good about

himself radiates an alluring aura. Paying attention to personal hygiene, grooming, and dressing appropriately communicates respect for yourself and those around you, signifying that you value the people you interact with, which is inherently attractive. Taking care of your appearance reflects an attention to detail, a highly appealing quality, as women often appreciate a man who is meticulous and thoughtful. Good grooming and maintaining your physique are not just about aesthetics; they also reflect a commitment to health and well-being, signaling to women that you are responsible and committed to taking care of yourself and those close to you. Your clothing and personal style can be a reflection of your personality and individuality, expressing your uniqueness and making you more interesting and appealing. Humans are sensory creatures, and being clean, well-groomed, and appropriately dressed can make you more visually and physically appealing, enhancing the overall sensory experience you provide.

First impressions matter, whether it's a first date or a chance encounter, and your appearance is the first thing people notice about you. Making a positive first impression sets the stage for further interactions and potential attraction. Shared values in personal care and grooming can be a sign of compatibility, and when you take care of your appearance, you often feel better about yourself, leading to a positive mood that can enhance your interactions with women. While initial attraction may be visual, long-term attraction often goes beyond looks, and a consistent effort in maintaining your appearance shows that you're committed to keeping the flame of attraction alive, even as a relationship progresses. Taking care of your appearance doesn't mean trying to fit a certain mold or obsessing over perfection; it's about embracing your unique qualities and presenting yourself in the best light, being comfortable in your skin, and allowing your appearance to reflect the confident and attractive person you are. When you take care of your appearance, you're not just making a statement about your external self; you're also making a statement about the kind of person you are on the inside – someone who is caring, considerate, and confident, all qualities that are highly attractive to women.

Get rid of the scarcity mentality and adopt the abundance mentality

Often, men find themselves falling into the trap of the scarcity mentality, which can lead to self-sabotaging behaviors. This mindset makes them believe that there are only a handful of opportunities, especially when it comes to forming meaningful connections with women. They start thinking, "There is NOBODY out there for me, so I better treat this one woman with absolute perfection because who knows when I'll ever experience something like this again."

This mindset is not about being modest; it's self-destructive. It chips away their self-worth and potential for happiness and success.

When you start thinking this way, you settle for relationships that may not truly fulfill you. You might start favoring anyone who remotely shows interest in you, convinced that you can't replicate that connection elsewhere. It's a trap that many men fall into without realizing it, resulting in relationships that are less than what they truly deserve. Cultivating an abundance mentality fundamentally boosts confidence. The belief that there are abundant opportunities to connect with remarkable women naturally imbues one with self-assuredness and charisma. Confidence is a magnetic trait that captivates and draws people in.

By relinquishing the scarcity mentality, men open the doors to authentic and meaningful connections. Rather than settling for relationships that fall short of their true desires, they approach interactions with a sense of curiosity and eagerness.

This allows them to seek compatibility and mutual growth, eliminating the need to settle for less due to perceived scarcity.

Moreover, men who embrace abundance tend to make more balanced and thoughtful decisions. They are less prone to rushing into relationships and making hasty choices because they no longer operate from a place of fear and anxiety.

Shedding the scarcity mentality also diminishes neediness. Neediness and clingy behavior often result from the fear of missing out on potential partners. By adopting an abundance mindset, men become less emotionally dependent and more likely to experience balanced, fulfilling relationships.

Optimism and positivity are natural byproducts of this shift in mindset. Believing in the abundance of opportunities fosters a brighter outlook and a sense of self-assuredness about one's potential to find a compatible partner. This positive attitude not only elevates mood but also makes men more attractive to others.Abundance encourages personal growth and learning through diverse relationship experiences. It allows for the exploration of different dynamics, a deeper understanding of personal preferences, and continuous refinement of one's approach to relationships.

Respecting women as individuals, rather than objects of scarcity, is a critical facet of adopting this mentality. An abundance mindset nurtures empathy and respect, leading to healthier, more considerate interactions. Additionally, this shift reduces the immense pressure placed on individual relationships. The scarcity mindset often burdens relationships with unrealistic expectations, stifling their growth. Embracing abundance lightens the load on each interaction, allowing them to develop more naturally and organically.

The solution lies in shifting from the scarcity mentality to the abundance mentality. The truth is, there isn't just one person in the world with whom you can share a deep connection. There are billions of women out there, each with unique qualities waiting to be explored. To get there, it's essential to stop placing women on pedestals. Treat them with respect, certainly, but also recognize your own worth and the abundance of opportunities that await when you do. It's about finding a balance, appreciating your uniqueness, and welcoming the vast possibilities that life offers in terms of connections and relationships.

I hope you are now able to understand women a little bit better and all the reasons why women have a tendency to always be drawn to bad boys even though they say they do not. Women's actions often do not correlate with their words. Thank you for reading :)

Reference:

Gangestad, S. W., Thornhill, R., & Garver-Apgar, C. E. (2016). Women's sexual interests across the ovulatory cycle. In D. M. Buss (Ed.), *The handbook of evolutionary psychology: Foundations* (pp. 403–426). John Wiley & Sons, Inc..

Gangestad, S. W., Thornhill, R., & Garver-Apgar, C. E. (2005). Women's sexual interests across the ovulatory cycle depend on primary partner developmental instability. *Proceedings. Biological sciences, 272*(1576), 2023–2027. https://doi.org/10.1098/rspb.2005.3112

Durante, K. M., & Arsena, A. R. (2015). Playing the Field: The Effect of Fertility on Women's Desire for Variety. *Journal of Consumer Research, 41*(6), 1372–1391. https://doi.org/10.1086/679652

About the author:

Camelia Khan is a dating coach and transformational expert, with an impressive track record of assisting hundreds of men in recent years. Her journey as a dating coach has been marked by a relentless passion for helping men revamp their dating lives, unlock their true potential, and embark on a transformative quest to become the best versions of themselves. With a profound understanding of the intricacies of dating and relationships, Camelia has been a guiding light for men seeking to navigate the complexities of the modern dating landscape. Her expertise extends far beyond mere dating advice; it encompasses the holistic development of men, helping them cultivate not only their dating skills but also their self-esteem and self-awareness.

At the core of Camelia's work is the unwavering belief that every man has the capacity to become the confident, captivating, and irresistible individual they aspire to be. Through her coaching, she empowers men to unleash their inner charisma, allowing them to connect with women on a deeper level, foster meaningful relationships, and ultimately find the love and connection they desire. Camelia Khan's dedication to her clients goes beyond conventional dating wisdom. Her approach is deeply rooted in the philosophy that authenticity is the cornerstone of true attraction. By guiding men to embrace their genuine selves, Camelia empowers them to create lasting and authentic connections with women. As an author, dating coach, and transformational mentor, Camelia Khan's work is not only about helping men understand the dating game but about equipping them with the tools and knowledge they need to thrive in the world of love and relationships. With her guidance, men embark on a journey of self-discovery and personal growth, emerging as more confident, captivating, and irresistible individuals. Camelia Khan's passion for transformation and her commitment to helping men find love and happiness make her a respected and sought-after figure in the realm of dating coaching. Her dedication to the success and happiness of her clients is a testament to her unwavering mission to make a positive impact in the lives of men seeking love, fulfillment, and connection.

Printed in Great Britain
by Amazon

37995466R00036